THE SURREY
COLOURING BOOK

First published 2017

The History Press
The Mill, Brimscombe Port
Stroud, Gloucestershire, GL5 2QG
www.thehistorypress.co.uk

ISBN 978 0 7509 8002 9

Typesetting and origination by The History Press
Printed and bound in Great Britain by TJ International Ltd

THE SURREY
COLOURING BOOK

PAST AND PRESENT

Take some time out of your busy life to relax and unwind with this feel-good colouring book designed for everyone who loves Surrey.

Absorb yourself in the simple action of colouring in the scenes and settings from around the county, past and present. From iconic architecture to picturesque vistas, you are sure to find some of your favourite locations waiting to be transformed with a splash of colour.

There are no rules – choose any page and any choice of colouring pens or pencils you like to create your own unique, colourful and creative illustrations.

University of Surrey ▶

Painshill Park Gothic Temple, Cobham ▸

Brooklands Aviation Museum ▸

Peacocks at Busbridge Lakes ▶

RHS Gardens, Wisley ▸

Guildford Cathedral interior ▶

The Savill Garden, Englefield Green ▸

The Sculpture Park, Churt ▸

Zodiac, Thorpe Park ▸

Watts Chapel, Artists' Village, Guildford ▶

London Bus Museum, Weybridge ▸

Priory Park, Reigate ▶

Guildford Museum ▶

Hampton Court Palace ▸

Camberley cricket ground, *c*. 1920 ▶

Hogs Back Brewery, Tongham ▸

Gostrey Meadow, Farnham ▶

Magna Carta memorial, Runnymede ▶

TO
COMMEMORATE
MAGNA CARTA
SYMBOL OF
FREEDOM
UNDER
LAW

The Cathedrals Express visits Addlestone Station ▶

Royal Holloway, Egham ▶

Sandown Park Racecourse, Esher ▸

Polesden Lacey ▶

Hannah Peschar Sculpture Garden, Ockley ▶

Rural Life Centre, Farnham ▸

Basingstoke Canal ▶

Loseley House and Gardens, Guildford ▶

Percival Sea Prince at Gatwick Aviation Museum, Charlwood ▸

Waverley Abbey, Farnham ▸

Shere village ▸

Honeywood Museum, Carshalton ▸

Greathed Manor, Dormansland ▸

Ockley cottages ▸

Gatton Park, Reigate ▸

The Anchor, Pyrford Lock, Woking ▸

Leatherhead, *c.* 1910 ▸

Rowing boats on the River Thames ▶

Cobham Mill ▸

Eashing Bridge, *c.* 1910 ▶

Dorking cockerel roundabout ▶

Lion & Lamb Yard, Farnham ▸

Red deer at the British Wildlife Centre, Lingfield ▸

Godalming ▸

Claremont Mansion, *c.* 1860 ▸

Sutton, *c.* 1910 ▶